Homemade
BIRD FOOD

DEDICATION

This book is dedicated to Elizabeth, Byron and Rachael. Wamlati!

ACKNOWLEDGMENTS

My sincere thanks to the countless volunteers who have contributed their time, energies and field data to breeding bird atlases, bird counts and other citizen science projects. The collaborative efforts of volunteers and wildlife professionals across North America, as well as globally important migratory wintering areas, provide vital information to the life histories and population status of birds. These resources have been imperative in the writing of the Wild About series of bird books.

Carrol Henderson, Supervisor, Minnesota DNR Nongame Wildlife Program: Thank you for reviewing the book and sharing your knowledge of North American birds. Your input has been invaluable.

Friends, the neighborhood gang, and the teachers and students who shared their ideas and support: Thank you for your incredible enthusiasm and imaginative input.

Helen and John Scuffham's Garden, Helen's Gourd Creations: Thank you for providing/preparing the incredible gourds for the feeders and for sharing your creative talents.

Cover and book design by Jonathan Norberg

Photo credits by photographer and page number:

Front cover photos: Banana Split, Happy Bird-day Cake, Sunflower Snack, Festive Outdoor Appetizers by Alan Stankevitz; appl-icious Crumble Pie by Jonathan Norberg

Back cover photos: Banana Split and Double-dipped Cone by Alan Stankevitz, Red-headed Woodpecker by Stan Tekiela

Jonathan Norberg: 9, 10 (cornmeal) **Alan Stankevitz:** 10 (sunflower chips), 11 (safflower), 27, 29, 31, 33, 34 (Summer Tanager), 35, 37, 39, 41, 42 (Brown Creeper), 43, 45, 46 (Summer Tanager), 47, 49, 51, 53, 55, 57, 59, 61, 63, 65, 67, 69, 71, 73, 75, 79 (Brown Creeper), 77 (Zebra-striped suet-sicle), 82 (Summer Tanager) **Stan Tekiela:** 34 (House Wren), 58 (American Black Duck), 70 (Red-headed Woodpecker), 78 (American Black Duck), 80 (House Wren), 81 (Red-headed Woodpecker) *credits continued on page 88*

10 9 8 7 6 5 4 3 2 1

Homemade Bird Food: 26 Fun & Easy Recipes to Feed Backyard Birds
First Edition 2010 (entitled *Cooking for the Birds*), Second Edition 2020
Copyright © 2010 and 2020 by Adele Porter
Published by Adventure Publications
An imprint of AdventureKEEN
330 Garfield Street South
Cambridge, Minnesota 55008
(800) 678-7006
www.adventurepublications.net
Printed in China
ISBN 978-1-59193-717-3 (pbk.)

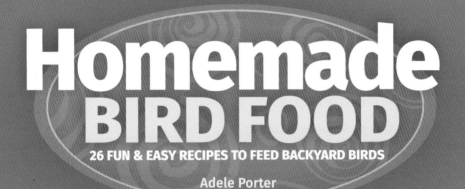

Homemade
BIRD FOOD
26 FUN & EASY RECIPES TO FEED BACKYARD BIRDS

Adele Porter

by Adele Porter

Adventure Publications
Cambridge, Minnesota

Table of Contents

Make Bird Food at Home

If you are wild about birds, then *Homemade Bird Food* will guide you in planning, preparing and hosting a backyard banquet for the birds. Designed for the entire family (ages 5–105), the 26 easy recipes in this book provide a banquet of nutritious food choices for a wide variety of backyard birds—from robins, woodpeckers and hummingbirds to chickadees and more! Once your buffet is served, sit back and enjoy the festivities. Contribute the information about the birds in your backyard, school yard or urban setting to a citizen science project that works toward the stewardship of our limited natural resources.

HOW TO USE THIS BOOK

Backyard bird feeding is like hosting a dinner party for wildlife. There are several stages involved in planning and implementing the whole affair. These stages are described in the following sections.

Set the Table for Success with an understanding of the foods birds eat, how food preferences vary by bird species and how a bird's nutritional needs vary according to season.

Cooking Basics will help you learn the basic ingredients of bird feeding.

Arrange the Dining Room with the help of tips for creating a backyard or urban habitat that attracts and meets the needs of wildlife. Then, create your banquet guest list from the seating chart.

Invite the Guests: Prepare the Menu by reviewing this list of the 75 most common North American backyard birds. This list is arranged by bird order and identifies the foods that each species is most attracted to in a feeder setting. It also identifies the region of the United States where the birds are most likely to inhabit. From this list you can plan your banquet menu by selecting the bird species you desire to attract and then preparing a recipe that matches the ingredients, or you can simply whip up a favorite recipe and prepare for guests to arrive.

Recipe Review provides a sample recipe to help you know what to expect.

Kids in the Kitchen features handy advice and safety tips for cooking when kids are in the kitchen.

Teaming Up: Citizen Science and Environmental Awareness are important, so once your banquet is served, find a comfortable seat and put on your citizen-science hat. You can be a part of ongoing science by contributing your bird information to a project sponsored by such groups as the National Audubon Society, the Cornell Lab of Ornithology and more.

Chef Notes at the end of this book are yours to fill in. You can keep track of the birds that are attracted to particular recipes, note changes you've made to a recipe, and create your own recipes from the ingredients list. Put your creativity to work and journal, sketch, keep a checklist of birds and more.

Homemade Bird Food blends kitchen and backyard science into a banquet of fun for wildlife enthusiasts of all ages. Let the feast begin!

SET THE TABLE FOR SUCCESS

Bird feeding is both a craft and a science. It can be as simple as setting out a sock feeder of thistle seeds and watching finches and chickadees feast. It may be as involved as understanding bird biology and the life histories of different species and then setting up feeders to attract specific birds in each season. This involves a full menu: insects for wrens, warblers and creepers; suet for nuthatches and woodpeckers; fruit for mockingbirds, orioles, cardinals and robins; acorns and other nuts scattered on the ground for Wild Turkeys and jays; and nectar for hummingbirds.

Bird feeding does not provide for a bird's total nutritional needs, but it supplements their diet of foods gained from the natural environment. This can be helpful during harsh winters. Black-capped Chickadees have been found to gain just over 20% of their overall nutrition from feeders. By setting up feeders and landscaping with plants that host natural food sources for wildlife, your yard can be an important part of providing for the basic needs of wildlife.

Seasonal Favorites

Each season provides an opportunity to set out food items that are suited to the specific needs of birds. For instance, neotropical migratory birds often feed on fruit in their South American winter homes, and when they come north to nest in North America they take advantage of the summer increase in mineral and protein-packed insects to fuel their chicks' fast growth.

WINTER: Birds that overwinter in the northern United States require high-calorie foods to produce enough heat to survive and to gain as many calories as possible while expending the least amount of energy. Fats and carbohydrates in the form of suet and nuts are on the winter menu along with calorie-laden sunflower and safflower seeds. Offering shelled nuts and seeds will also save birds the effort of opening the seeds.

SPRING/FALL: Fueling Migration The migratory movements of birds are triggered by changes in the length of daylight. During migration, birds produce additional hormones, allowing them to store energy in extra fat deposits; this energy is needed to fuel migratory flight. Migration is also the time of year when the widest variety of bird species pass through many areas. Provide a wide variety of food types and sizes at all habitat levels to attract these migrating birds.

In the spring, provide warblers with mealworms, and set out fruit, jelly, and nectar for orioles, catbirds and robins, along with the regular menu of seeds and nuts. Set out nectar and jelly feeders by May 1st in regions where birds are moving through on spring migration.

In the fall, set out high-calorie foods like nectar, suet and protein-rich items such as mealworms. Studies have indicated that feeding birds during migration has not been found to delay their normal departure schedules.

SUMMER: Nesting and Raising Young Feeding a nest full of young birds requires parents to spend their energy in searching, capturing and delivering food. The fast growth of young birds is fueled by large amounts of protein. Setting out mealworms along with the regular fare provides a ready source of protein for bird parents and their ravenous fledglings. Setting out eggshells offers female birds a source of replacement for the calcium that their body used to produce a clutch of eggs.

Providing suet and peanut butter on warm summer days can be a sticky situation for birds. The melted mixture can stick to and affect a bird's feathers, and consequently their eggs and young. Replacing suet and peanut butter with shelled, unshelled peanuts and peanut hearts provides a variety of pea-nutty treats for birds during the summer.

COOKING BASICS

The recipes in this cookbook call for ingredients common to bird feeding and cater to a wide variety of birds. Careful attention has been given to include only ingredients that are healthy for birds to ingest. The recipes have been built around these base ingredients so you can select a bird species you would like to attract, pair the food it eats with a recipe and then serve the resulting food in an appropriate type of feeder placed at the habitat level where the bird lives.

Get to know the ingredients and the recipes will be as easy as A, B, C.

Suet

Suet is lard/fat generally from beef, deer or other wild game. Suet can be served up as it is straight from the host animal or as it comes packaged from your local butcher. Chickadees will pick the rib cage of a deer carcass clean making for a ready-made bird feeder.

Suet can also be warmed and melted into a softer composition more easily managed for working into recipes. Caution is necessary when melting suet as it can flame at too high of a temperature; **this is a task for adults only**.

Although suet can be provided and eaten by birds in all seasons, it can become rancid during periods of warm weather. Consider substituting peanuts and peanut hearts during warm months of the year.

Suet Base Recipe

5 lb. of ground suet (ask your local meat department personnel to grind the suet for you).

Place half of the suet in a heavy pan over low heat*. For the purposes of this recipe, low is considered 2 in a heat range of 1–10. Stir the suet occasionally until it is in a semi-clear and liquid form. This generally takes about 15 minutes. Remove from the heat.

To remove any fibers, pour the suet through a fine wire mesh strainer into an 8 inch by 8 inch baking dish or like-sized plastic container with a lid for storing. Place the strained suet in the refrigerator until it is no longer clear and has hardened.

From this suet base, a wide variety of ingredients can be added to attract specific species of birds: seeds, nuts, dried fruit (fruity suet), peanut butter (pea-nutty suet), cornmeal, oatmeal and even dried mealworms for extra protein. For the best results, prepare with a ratio of two parts suet to one part extra ingredients.

Cornmeal

Cornmeal is finely ground corn used in baking quick breads, as coatings for meats and vegetables and in stuffing. Many birds are attracted to and benefit from the nutrients in cornmeal. Cornmeal is used as a substitute for white flour (wheat) in the recipes of this book. Some birds do not have the ability to digest white flour and it has little nutritional value for birds.

Black Oil Sunflower Seeds

Black oil sunflowers are commercially grown for pressing into sunflower oil. They are thin-shelled and easy for birds to hull. This is one of the most popular seeds at backyard feeders, attracting some 40 species of birds, including chickadees, goldfinches and titmice.

Striped Sunflower Seeds

Larger than black oil sunflower seeds and with less oil content, striped sunflower seeds are commercially grown for uses other than oil. This includes the sunflower snacks that we eat! Cardinals, grosbeaks, Purple Finches and nuthatches are just a few of the many birds that eat striped sunflowers.

Sunflower Seed Chips

Sunflower seed chips are eaten by smaller birds like chickadees, titmice, White-throated Sparrows and American Goldfinches. There are no hulls to clean up and very little seed is wasted.

Nyjer Seed

American Goldfinches are late nesters that take advantage of wild thistle seed to feed their young. Nyjer thistle is a commercial seed grown in India and Ethiopia for use in bird feeding. The seeds are very small and fine—just right for the small bills of finches, siskins, redpolls and even Indigo Buntings.

Safflower

Safflower is a plant that produces a flower head with seeds that are commercially grown for cooking oil. The seeds are eaten by Northern Cardinals, chickadees, doves and many other birds, but not by squirrels!

Proso Millet

White Proso millet is the small seed of the grass *Panicum miliaceum*. Millet is rich in B vitamins, calcium, potassium and zinc. It's popular with doves, finches, sparrows and juncos.

Cracked & Shelled Corn

Corn is high in carbohydrates, which fuel metabolism and make for a ready source of energy. Many birds eat corn, whether as meal, cracked, or shelled, including jays, doves, juncos, sparrows, blackbirds, Red-headed and Red-bellied Woodpeckers, Ring-necked Pheasants, Wild Turkeys, Northern Bobwhite, Mallards and Common Ravens.

Peanuts

Peanuts are a powerhouse of protein, minerals and vitamins B and E, and are a favorite of jays, woodpeckers, nuthatches, titmice and chickadees. Peanut hearts and chips are preferred by the smaller bird species.

Tree Nuts

Acorns, hickory nuts, hazelnuts and other tree nuts provide essential protein and oils to forest birds like Wild Turkeys, jays and woodpeckers.

Dried Fruit

Birds that eat fruit all year take advantage of wild berries dried on the vine or plant. Backyard birds especially like raisins, cranberries and other fruit plumped by soaking in orange juice; these include bluebirds, robins, mockingbirds, cardinals, catbirds, thrashers, White-crowned Sparrows and tanagers.

ARRANGE THE DINING ROOM

In a bird's-eye view the natural world is a dining room and your yard is one part of the larger landscape. One of North America's most common birds, the American

Rooftop Garden

Robin, requires about one-half of an acre to as much as 2 acres for its breeding territory. Your yard or common area may not be this large, but when you consider the big picture of neighboring yards and public areas, the needs of robins and many other birds and wildlife can be met. Providing year-round food, water and shelter with a variety of plants, ground covers and trees will attract a variety of birds in all seasons.

- Invite birds to your yard by providing shelter and a place to nest and raise their young. Build and set out bird nesting and roosting structures, and provide nesting materials in the spring. Consider leaving older trees with hollow cavities or those with the potential for birds to excavate cavities. Many species of wildlife depend on older trees. Leave stumps for stump feeders, too.

- Landscape your yard with fruit-bearing trees and shrubs, and flowering plants with blooms spread throughout the growing season. A diversity of plantings in your yard will attract an equally diverse array of wildlife.

- Birds have adapted to eating foods at different levels of a habitat. Making a range of foods available at all habitat levels will attract a wide variety of birds to your backyard dining room.

- Include the sound of moving or dripping water. Provide a source of clean water all year. Refreshing the water in a bird bath at least once per week will keep algal growth in check and mosquito larvae from developing. There are bird water heaters available for use in northern areas during winter months.

- Keep the food fresh. Rancid or moldy food is unhealthy for birds. Clean your feeders with a solution of one part bleach to nine parts water several times per year.

- Arrange hanging feeders in stations of 3–5 feeders, but don't put too many feeders close together. Overcrowding can create unhealthy conditions.

- Set bird feeders in predator-free areas with some open space where birds can cue in on any movement of a predator. Some birds, like those that spend their time foraging for food on the ground, feel comfortable with a brush pile near a ground feeding station where they can find immediate cover. Keep cats indoors.

- Life exchanges for life in a continuous cycle. Your backyard is a part of this energy chain. While songbirds are feasting at your backyard banquet, they may become a meal for a Sharp-shinned Hawk or a Cooper's Hawk. These small, slender-bodied woodland hawks maneuver around trees with their short, rounded wings and long tails. Both species are gray above and light below with reddish bars. They have red eyes and long, yellow legs.

- To discourage hawks from dining on the smaller birds at your feeders, discontinue filling the feeders for a few weeks. The smaller birds will find food in natural areas with more cover and the hawk will move to another area. Resume feeding when the pattern has been broken and backyard birds are no longer an á la carte item for hawks.

- The stewardship of natural resources extends to our shared and individual home outdoor spaces. Pesticides and herbicides applied to lawns and gardens find their way through the food chain and can adversely affect wildlife at all levels. Children playing in these environments are exposed as well. Healthy lawn-care alternatives are available; check with your local Extension service for advice.

- Be consistent. Be patient. Birds may start to show up in as little as a few days or it may take a season or two for some bird species to arrive. However long it takes, it is sure to be well worth the wait!

Cedar Waxwing

INVITE THE GUESTS: PREPARE THE MENU

Planning a backyard banquet requires a guest list and a menu. Decide on which guests to invite by identifying the birds that inhabit your region of North America. The 75 common North American backyard and waterside birds in this list are arranged taxonomically, by bird order, and are identified as occurring in the Northern US (N), the Southern US (S), the Eastern half of the country (E), the Western half of the country (W), or a combination of East and West (E/W). These ranges are only approximate, so consult a field guide to find the specific birds near you. For the purposes of this book, the Mississippi River is the dividing line between east and west, and the 40th parallel north divides north and south.

It's easy to prepare the menu for your guests if you know their food preferences. Each bird species has adapted to eat certain foods; some eat only insects or fruit or seeds, and others eat a variety of foods. Only the foods a bird species commonly eats at a backyard feeder or waterside park are included in this list. You can also use this as a checklist for recording the birds that come to dine at your school, urban or backyard buffet.

Birds & Their Order	Seeds & Nuts	Fruit	Insects	Suet	Sap	Nectar
Anseriformes: Swans, Geese, Ducks						
Canada Goose (E/W)*	🐦					
Wood Duck (E/W)*	🐦					
Mallard (E/W)*	🐦					
American Black Duck (E/W)*	🐦					
Galliformes: Pheasants, Grouse, Quails, Turkeys						
Ring-necked Pheasant (E/W)	🐦		🐦	🐦		
Northern Bobwhite (N/E)	🐦		🐦	🐦		
Wild Turkey (E/W)	🐦		🐦	🐦		
Columbiformes: Pigeons & Doves						
Rock Pigeon (E/W)	🐦					
Mourning Dove (E/W)	🐦					

* Found only near waterside parks

14

Birds & Their Order	Seeds & Nuts	Fruit	Insects	Suet	Sap	Nectar
Apodiformes: Swifts & Hummingbirds						
Ruby-throated Hummingbird (E)			🐦		🐦	🐦
Anna's Hummingbird (W)						🐦
Rufous Hummingbird (W)						🐦
Black-chinned Hummingbird (W)						🐦
Piciformes: Woodpeckers & Allies						
Red-headed Woodpecker (E/W)	🐦	🐦	🐦	🐦		
Red-bellied Woodpecker (E)	🐦	🐦	🐦	🐦		
Yellow-bellied Sapsucker (E/W)	🐦	🐦	🐦	🐦	🐦	🐦
Downy Woodpecker (E/W)	🐦	🐦	🐦	🐦		🐦
Hairy Woodpecker (E/W)	🐦	🐦	🐦	🐦		🐦
Northern Flicker (E/W)		🐦	🐦	🐦		
Pileated Woodpecker (E)			🐦	🐦		
Passeriformes: Perching Birds						
Gray Jay (N)	🐦	🐦	🐦	🐦	🐦	
Steller's Jay (W)	🐦	🐦	🐦			
Blue Jay (E/W)	🐦	🐦	🐦	🐦		
Western Scrub Jay (W)	🐦	🐦	🐦			
Black-billed Magpie (W)	🐦		🐦	🐦		
Purple Martin (E/W)	EGGSHELLS ONLY					
Carolina Chickadee (E)	🐦	🐦	🐦	🐦		
Black-capped Chickadee (E/W)	🐦	🐦	🐦	🐦		
Mountain Chickadee (W)	🐦	🐦	🐦			
Boreal Chickadee (N)		🐦		🐦		
Tufted Titmouse (E)	🐦		🐦	🐦		
Bushtit (W)			🐦			

Birds & Their Order	Seeds & Nuts	Fruit	Insects	Suet	Sap	Nectar
Red-breasted Nuthatch (E/W)	●		●	●	●	
White-breasted Nuthatch (E/W)	●		●	●	●	
Brown Creeper (N)			●	●		●
Carolina Wren (E)			●	●		
House Wren (E)			●			
Golden-crowned Kinglet (N)	●		●			
Ruby-crowned Kinglet (N/W)	●		●	●		
Western Bluebird (W)			●			
Eastern Bluebird (E)			●			
American Robin (E/W)	●	●	●			
Gray Catbird (E/W)	●	●	●	●		
Northern Mockingbird (E/W)	●	●	●	●		
Brown Thrasher (E)	●	●	●	●		
Bohemian Waxwing (W)		●	●			
Cedar Waxwing (E)		●	●			
Yellow-rumped Warbler (E/W)			●	●		
Ovenbird (E)			●			
Spotted Towhee (W)	●	●	●			
Eastern Towhee (E)	●	●	●	●		●
Chipping Sparrow (E/W)	●		●			
Fox Sparrow (E/W)	●	●	●			
Song Sparrow (E/W)	●		●			
White-throated Sparrow (E)	●	●	●			
White-crowned Sparrow (E/W)	●		●			
Golden-crowned Sparrow (W)	●		●			
Dark-eyed Junco (E/W)	●		●			
Summer Tanager (E/W)	●	●	●			●
Scarlet Tanager (S/E)		●	●	●		

Birds & Their Order	Seeds & Nuts	Fruit	Insects	Suet	Sap	Nectar
Northern Cardinal (E/W)	✓	✓	✓			
Black-headed Grosbeak (W)	✓	✓	✓			
Rose-breasted Grosbeak (E)	✓		✓			
Indigo Bunting (E/W)	✓		✓			
Bullock's Oriole (W)	✓	✓	✓	✓		✓
Baltimore Oriole (E)	✓	✓	✓	✓		✓
Pine Grosbeak (W)	✓		✓	✓		
Purple Finch (E/W)	✓		✓			
Cassin's Finch (W)	✓					
House Finch (E/W)	✓	✓	✓			
Common Redpoll (E/W)			✓	✓		
Pine Siskin (E/W)	✓					
Lesser Goldfinch (W)	✓					
American Goldfinch (E/W)	✓					
Evening Grosbeak (E/W)	✓		✓			

Ingredients
The base ingredients of the recipe.

Tools
A list of items required to prepare the recipe that are outside of standard cooking equipment. Basic kitchen supplies (bowl, spoon, etc.) are not included in the list.

Happy Bird-day Cake

INGREDIENTS

1 cup oatmeal, coarsely ground in food processor
¼ cup cornmeal
½ teaspoon baking powder
1 tablespoon Nyjer seed
1 tablespoon sunflower chips
1 egg
½ cup milk or water, warmed
2 tablespoons melted suet
⅓ cup Raisin-berry Relish (page 60), or raisins and cranberries
Toppings: peanut butter, nuts, seeds, carrot sticks and pumpkin seeds

TOOLS

Muffin tin and liners
Food processor

DIRECTIONS

STEP 1
Preheat the oven to 350°F. Line a muffin tin with paper liners. Set aside.

STEP 2
Combine the coarsely ground oatmeal, cornmeal, baking powder, seeds and sunflower chips in a medium mixing bowl. Make a well in the center.

STEP 3
Whip the egg in a separate bowl. Add the warmed milk or water, melted suet and then the Raisin-berry Relish.

STEP 4
Pour the egg mixture into the well in the center of the oatmeal-nut mixture. Stir until ingredients are combined, but do not overmix. Fill muffin cups ⅔ full.

STEP 5
Bake for 20 minutes or until lightly browned and a toothpick inserted in the center comes out clean. Cool. Frost with peanut butter and decorate with seeds, nuts and dried mealworms. Top with a carrot candle with a pumpkin-seed flame.

Directions
Each recipe is written in three to five easy steps.

Time
Most recipes require 30–40 minutes or less to prepare.

Attracts
Look to this space for four featured species that may come to eat this completed food recipe.

ATTRACTS

40

 White-breasted Nuthatch

 Northern Cardinal

 Downy Woodpecker

 Evening Grosbeak

RECIPE REVIEW

The 26 recipes in *Homemade Bird Food* are presented in an easy-to-follow format that provides recipe directions, helpful hints, guest list possibilities, birding background and ideas on how to present the completed recipes to your backyard guests. Get to know the recipe layout and you will be wild about cooking for the birds!

NOTES

Celebrate the birds in your backyard with a cake. How many candles do birds have on their bird-day cake? For most birds, the first six months are the most perilous. In perching birds (Passerines), once the young have survived their first six months, they may have one, two, three, or as many as six birthdays. There are exceptional individual birds, however, like an American Robin that lived nearly 14 years!

ALSO ATTRACTS: Black-headed Grosbeak; Hairy Woodpecker; Blue Jay; Northern Mockingbird; Gray Catbird

This recipe can be divided into individual cake tins, baked and frozen until needed.

Tip
Includes hints on the use of the recipes, interesting bird science, ways to deter other wildlife like squirrels and more!

41

Notes
Interesting natural history information, bird watching and bird feeding tips, recipe ideas and ideas on landscaping with natural plant foods.

Also Attracts
A sampling of even more bird species that may come to eat this completed recipe.

RECIPE OPTIONS

Use this chart to determine which recipes to make for certain species, or to determine which birds might be attracted to a recipe you'd like to make.

Species	Appl-icious Crumble Pie	Banana Split	Coconut Café	Double-dipped Cone	Eggshell Salad	Festive Outdoor Appetizers	Gobbler Goulash	Happy Bird-day Cake	Irresistible Insects	Jelly Deli
American Black Duck (E/W)*										
American Goldfinch (E/W)										
American Robin (E/W)	●								●	
Anna's Hummingbird (W)										
Baltimore Oriole (E)	●							●	●	
Black-billed Magpie (W)		●								
Black-capped Chickadee (E/W)			●	●		●		●		
Black-chinned Hummingbird (W)										
Black-headed Grosbeak (W)										
Blue Jay (E/W)	●				●	●	●		●	
Bohemian Waxwing (W)										
Boreal Chickadee (N)			●							
Brown Creeper (N)								●		
Brown Thrasher (E)										
Bullock's Oriole (W)										
Bushtit (W)								●		
Canada Goose (E/W)*										
Carolina Chickadee (E)			●		●					
Carolina Wren (E)				●					●	
Cassin's Finch (W)										
Cedar Waxwing (E)										
Chipping Sparrow (E/W)							●	●		
Common Redpoll (E/W)										
Dark-eyed Junco (E/W)					●					
Downy Woodpecker (E/W)		●		●				●		
Eastern Bluebird (E)		●		●				●		
Eastern Towhee (E)		●			●				●	
Evening Grosbeak (E/W)						●	●			
Fox Sparrow (E/W)										
Golden-crowned Kinglet (N)								●		
Golden-crowned Sparrow (W)		●								
Gray Catbird (E/W)	●				●		●			
Gray Jay (N)	●				●				●	
Hairy Woodpecker (E/W)		●		●	●	●	●			
House Finch (E/W)		●								
House Wren (E)				●				●		
Indigo Bunting (E/W)								●		
Lesser Goldfinch (W)										
Mallard (E/W)*										
Mountain Chickadee (W)		●		●	●			●		

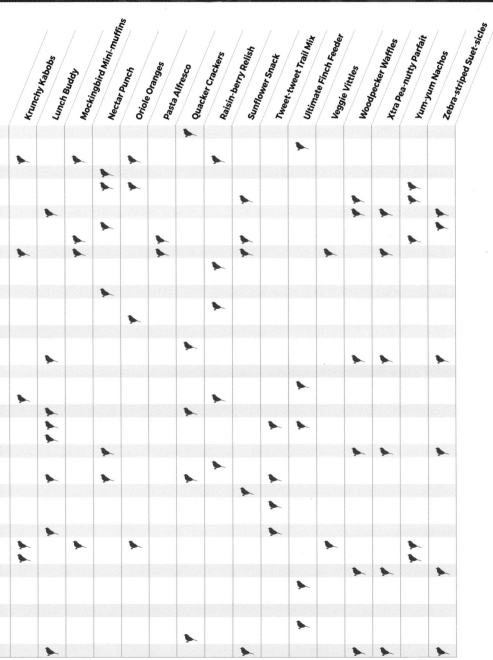

* Found only near waterside parks

	Appl-icious Crumble Pie	Banana Split	Coconut Café	Double-dipped Cone	Eggshell Salad	Festive Outdoor Appetizers	Gobbler Goulash	Happy Bird-day Cake	Irresistible Insects	Jelly Deli
Mourning Dove (E/W)	●						●			
Northern Bobwhite (N/E)	●						●			
Northern Cardinal (E/W)			●		●			●		
Northern Flicker (E/W)		●								
Northern Mockingbird (E/W)	●					●		●	●	
Ovenbird (E)					●			●		
Pileated Woodpecker (E)						●				
Pine Grosbeak (W)			●							
Pine Siskin (E/W)										
Purple Finch (E/W)										
Purple Martin (E/W)				●						
Red-bellied Woodpecker (E)	●	●				●				
Red-breasted Nuthatch (E/W)		●	●	●						
Red-headed Woodpecker (E/W)		●				●				
Ring-necked Pheasant (E/W)							●			
Rock Pigeon (E/W)			●				●			
Rose-breasted Grosbeak (E)			●							
Ruby-crowned Kinglet (N/W)									●	
Ruby-throated Hummingbird (E)										
Rufous Hummingbird (W)										
Scarlet Tanager (S/E)				●						
Song Sparrow (E/W)										
Spotted Towhee (W)	●		●							
Steller's Jay (W)					●					
Summer Tanager E/W)					●				●	
Tufted Titmouse (E)		●		●	●					
Western Bluebird (W)								●		
Western Scrub Jay (W)				●						
White-breasted Nuthatch (E/W)		●	●	●		●		●	●	
White-crowned Sparrow (E/W)										
White-throated Sparrow (E)			●							
Wild Turkey (E/W)							●			
Wood Duck (E/W)*							●			
Yellow-bellied Sapsucker (E/W)	●	●				●				
Yellow-rumped Warbler (E/W)		●						●		

22

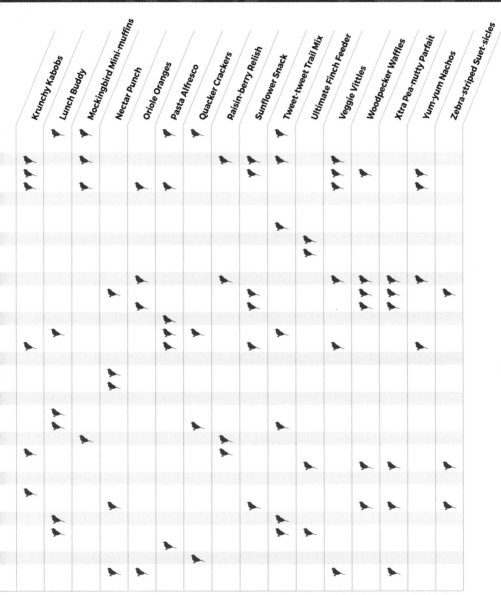

* Found only near waterside parks

KIDS IN THE KITCHEN

Cooking with your child is a fun way to spend time together while building essential life-long skills. The recipes in this cookbook are intended for adults and for children, with the premise that parents know best the unique capabilities of their child and what constitutes a safe level of engagement.

For kids, cooking in a kitchen can be a lot like doing a fun science experiment in a chemistry lab. It's fascinating to mix ingredients and see the reaction. Your goal is to make sure that the reactions occur as planned, so here are a few simple tips to make certain that kitchen science remains fun and safe.

- Read the directions thoroughly before starting. Modeling this essential rule of cooking will prepare your child for any steps that require your absolute supervision.

- When the recipe calls for the use of a knife, electrical appliance and/or heat, an adult should be in charge.

- Remind your young assistant to keep electrical cords and appliances away from contact with water.

- Keep any loose clothing, jewelry or hair away from moving parts and heat. Tie back long hair and remove jewelry. Roll up your sleeves, put on an apron and get ready to safely cook!

- Always be sure to wash your hands before and after cooking!

Hint: Cooking can bring on hunger for kids. Provide them with kid-sized portions of fruit, vegetables and nuts in a separate part of the kitchen from the ingredients being used to cook for the birds. Explain that the food they are cooking is not for people, even though some of the ingredients are familiar.

TEAMING UP: CITIZEN SCIENCE AND ENVIRONMENTAL AWARENESS

With birds feasting at your banquet, it's time for action. You can contribute your backyard bird data to ongoing wildlife research by participating in the following citizen science projects. You can make a difference toward the stewardship of natural resources!

Christmas/Holiday Bird Count	www.audubon.org/conservation/science/christmas-bird-count
Great Backyard Bird Count	www.birdsource.org/gbbcApps/kids
Journey North	www.learner.org/jnorth
Project Feeder Watch	www.birds.cornell.edu/pfw/
Celebrate Urban Birds	https://celebrateurbanbirds.org/
eBird	https://ebird.org/home

Enhance Your Birding Experience with These Journals

- Note which birds you see
- Track when and where you saw them
- Enjoy bonus activities and information

Appl-icious Crumble Pie

INGREDIENTS

Half an apple
1 cup cornmeal
1 tablespoon thistle seed
1 tablespoon millet seed
1 tablespoon sunflower chips
½ cup suet base
½ cup grape jelly

TOOLS

Mini-pie pan

DIRECTIONS

STEP 1

Slice the apple into thin wedges and then cut them in half. Set aside for later. Combine cornmeal, thistle, millet and sunflower chips with the suet base in a mixing bowl. Use your hands to work in to a crumble. If the mixture is too stiff, simply warm it in the microwave. Press the mixture into the sides and bottom of a mini-pie pan. Place pie shell in the refrigerator. Cool until hard.

STEP 2

Place the jelly in a small saucepan over low heat. Stir until melted. Remove from heat. Pour the melted jelly into the cooled pie shell, filling it half full.

STEP 3

Arrange the apple slices in a circle. Chill in a refrigerator for several hours or overnight. Optional garnish: Crumble extra crust mixture on the top and place a cherry in the middle.

STEP 4

To release the pie from the pan, turn it over and tap the bottom. If the pie does not come out, place the very bottom of the pie pan in a sink of shallow warm water for 30 seconds and then try again. The pie may be served in the pan, also.

ATTRACTS

American Robin

Gray Catbird

Mourning Dove

Baltimore Oriole

female Baltimore Oriole

NOTES

The American Robins in your yard eat more than worms; they love apples! Last summer, a bold male robin came regularly to my backyard to eat chopped apples followed by a second course of grapes.

He topped his afternoon snack by cooling off in the water sprinkler. Whip up this appl-icious crumble pie and prepare for hungry robins, catbirds, cardinals, doves, orioles and more!

ALSO ATTRACTS: Spotted Towhee; Northern Mockingbird; Gray and Blue Jays; Yellow-bellied Sapsucker; Red-bellied Woodpecker; Bullock's Oriole

To serve your guests, place the pie in a backyard location away from cats and squirrels. Serve the pie near an oriole nectar feeder and attract Baltimore Orioles too!

Banana Split

INGREDIENTS

1 peeled banana
Two small scoops of suet base,
  suet-fruit combo, or nutty suet
Half an orange, peeled and
  cut into pieces
Handful of grapes, halved
2 cherries
Shelled peanuts or other seeds
1 crushed eggshell
¼ cup of grape jelly
Live mealworms (optional—but the warblers and bluebirds would say required!)

TOOLS

Ice cream scoop
Banana split dish or
  recycled container

DIRECTIONS

STEP 1

Slice the banana in half lengthwise and place both halves in a dish that can be kept outside. (Secondhand stores often have banana split dishes for sale, or be creative and recycle a leftover container.)

STEP 2

Place two scoops of suet base between the banana halves. (Hint: Warm the scoop in hot water to allow it to scoop and release the suet more easily.)

STEP 3

Heat the jelly until it is melted. Drizzle the jelly over the mounds of suet.

STEP 4

Place the fruit pieces, nuts and seeds around the suet. During winter in northern regions, substitute peanuts and other nuts and seeds for the fruit.

STEP 5

Sprinkle the crushed eggshell and squirmy mealworms on top.

ATTRACTS

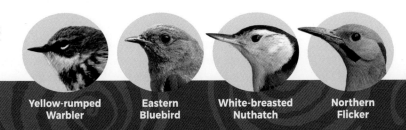

Yellow-rumped
Warbler

Eastern
Bluebird

White-breasted
Nuthatch

Northern
Flicker

female and male Eastern Bluebirds

NOTES

Just as dessert is only one part of a meal, the food eaten by backyard birds is only a supplement to their full energy requirements. Research indicates that just over 20% of the winter energy needs of chickadees are gained from food sources at bird feeding stations. Fill the water glasses (bird baths) all year, too. Birds fulfill their water needs from direct sources like puddles and bird feeders and from indirect sources such as the moisture content in foods and from respiration. Mourning Doves must visit a water source at least once per day. Bring on the feast!

ALSO ATTRACTS: Black-billed Magpie; Tufted Titmouse; Red-breasted Nuthatch; Eastern Towhee; Yellow-bellied Sapsucker; Downy, Hairy, Red-bellied and Red-headed Woodpeckers; Mountain Chickadee

Place the banana split on a tree stump or another elevated stand near tree branches (but not accessible to roaming cats and squirrels) in the spring and fall when warblers are migrating. Eastern Bluebirds will eat from this protein-packed meal during the summer nesting season.

Coconut Café

INGREDIENTS
1 Coconut

TOOLS
Drill
Woodworking saw
3 lengths of twine
Screw-eye (optional)

DIRECTIONS

STEP 1
This project works best with an assistant to help hold the coconut. Drill 3 holes in the base of the coconut. Drain the coconut water into a glass. You can drink it or save for other use.

STEP 2
Hold the coconut upright. Use the saw to cut straight down from the top of the coconut, as if cutting in half from top to bottom—but only cut halfway down, to the center of the coconut.

STEP 3
Turn the coconut on its side. Starting at the top, cut halfway down, meeting the first cut in the center of the coconut.

STEP 4
Clean the coconut meat out of the bottom half of the coconut. Set aside to eat or for later use.

STEP 5
Thread the twine through one hole and make a knot on the end inside the coconut. Repeat this with the other 2 lengths of twine, and then tie their ends together. Option: Screw a screw-eye into the top of the coconut and loop a length of twine through it for hanging the coconut feeder.

ATTRACTS

Black-capped Chickadee **Rose-breasted Grosbeak** **House Finch** **Red-breasted Nuthatch**

White-breasted Nuthatch

NOTES

Bird feeders can be made of many natural items—gourds, hollowed tree stumps and limbs, and even coconuts. While some birds are eating the seeds inside the coconut feeder, other birds pull the fibers from the outer shell for nesting materials. This feeder can be made with either half of a coconut or, as in the directions, with the full coconut for a feeder with a roof.

ALSO ATTRACTS: Spotted Towhee; Rock Pigeon; Northern Cardinal; White-throated and Golden-crowned Sparrows; Pine Grosbeak; White Breasted Nuthatch

Fill the coconut feeder with Tweet-tweet Trail Mix (page 64) or with suet base, fruity suet, or Xtra Pea-nutty Parfait (page 72). Hang this snazzy feeder in your yard and watch for birds to take their turns snacking at the Coconut Café.

Double-dipped Cone

INGREDIENTS
Pine cones
Suet
Seeds, any combination
Peanut butter

TOOLS
String or yarn

DIRECTIONS

STEP 1
Explore an area with pine trees and collect a few pine cones. Take time to enjoy the smell of pine needles underfoot and the activity of wildlife.

STEP 2
Tie a 12-inch length of string or yarn under the top layer of scales on the pine cone, just under the stem.

STEP 3
Melt suet on low heat in a heavy saucepan or double boiler. Hold onto the string and dip the cone into the melted suet. If the suet is not deep enough for dipping, pour suet over the cone with a long-handled spoon. (Hint: Place wax paper on a countertop to catch any drips.)

STEP 4
Immediately sprinkle seeds of your choice over the dipped cone. Let the cone cool on the waxed paper. To speed the cooling process, put the dipped cone in the refrigerator.

STEP 5
Heat the peanut butter in a microwave until it is melted. This will only take about 3 ten-second intervals. Immediately dip the cone into, or drizzle the melted peanut butter over, the cooled cone. Hang the cones outside and wait for hungry birds to dip in.

ATTRACTS

Black-capped Chickadee **Tufted Titmouse** **Hairy Woodpecker** **White-breasted Nuthatch**

NOTES

Seeds come packaged in very unique ways. Pine tree seeds are protected inside of pine cones. When a mature cone is exposed to heat, the individual sections spread open and the seeds eventually fall to the forest floor. Birds like Pine Siskins, and White-winged and Red Crossbills have bills uniquely shaped to remove and eat seeds from an opened pine cone. Make this recipe and watch for a variety of bird species to dip into a delicious snack right before your eyes.

ALSO ATTRACTS: Boreal, Carolina and Mountain Chickadees; Downy Woodpecker; Red-breasted Nuthatch

Eggshell Salad

INGREDIENTS

2–6 eggs
Quarter of a coconut shell,
  leftover from making
  Coconut Café (page 30)

TOOLS

3-foot-long ½-inch-diameter
  wood dowel
Hot glue or other glue
Drill

DIRECTIONS

STEP 1

Preheat oven to 275°F. Boil the eggs in a medium pan of water for seven minutes. Remove the eggs from the water with a slotted spoon and cool.

STEP 2

Peel the eggs, keeping the shells to one side for the birds.

STEP 3

Heat the eggshells in the oven for 15–20 minutes. This will rid the shells of any harmful bacteria. Cool. Crush the eggshells to the size of dry oatmeal flakes. Eggshells can be stored for adding to other recipes in this book and for refilling your saucer feeder.

STEP 4

To make an easy saucer feeder, clean the meat from the coconut shell. Drill a ½-inch hole in the center of the shell. Glue the end of the dowel into the hole. For a hanging feeder, drill a hole in the end of each side of the coconut shell and place a length of twine through each hole. Tie the ends of the twine together at the top for use in hanging the feeder.

STEP 5

Place the saucer feeder in your garden or yard and fill it with crushed eggshells and some sand for additional grit. Eggshell Salad is a great side dish in your backyard banquet!

ATTRACTS

House
Wren

Dark-eyed
Junco

Purple
Martin

Summer
Tanager

NOTES

The eggshells of birds are made of minerals, including calcium in the form of calcite crystals. Some bird parents eat the eggshells soon after the chicks hatch. This keeps the nest tidy, helps to keep predators from the nest and, in an adult female bird, replaces the calcium her body used to produce a clutch of eggs. Birds also need grit to aid in breaking down food. Eggshells and snail shells are eaten for both the calcium and the grit by birds like House Wrens. Set out eggshells in the spring and summer and watch the eggs-traordinary visits of busy backyard birds. At least 57 species of North American birds consume eggshells.

ALSO ATTRACTS: Carolina Wren; Blue, Steller's and Western Scrub Jays; Eastern Bluebird; Ovenbird; Northern Cardinal; Scarlet Tanager; Purple Martin

To provide extra grit, add some crushed snail shells to the eggshell salad.
Watch for wrens, martins, tanagers, warblers and juncos.

Festive Outdoor Appetizers

INGREDIENTS

Suet base
Cornmeal (optional)
Assorted seeds
Raisins and dried or
fresh cranberries

TOOLS

Assorted gelatin molds, ice cube tray,
or mini-muffin tin
Ribbon, raffia, twine, or string

DIRECTIONS

STEP 1

Mix a full recipe of plain, pea-nutty, or fruity suet following the directions on page 9. Cornmeal may be added at a ratio of 1 part cornmeal to 2 parts suet base.

STEP 2

Arrange raisins and cranberries in festive patterns in the bottom of individual molds. Next, press the suet firmly into the mold so there are no spaces in the mixture. A hole for hanging the appetizers can be made by placing a piece of macaroni into the mixture, one-third of the distance from the top, or insert a pipe cleaner into the suet to create a hook for hanging. Refrigerate until the mixture is hard. (Hint: A mini-muffin baking tin or ice cube tray can also be used. Place the end of a length of yarn, string, or raffia into the bottom before filling, to use for hanging, later.)

STEP 3

To release the ornament from the mold, place the base of the mold in a shallow sink of warm water. Tip the mold and tap the bottom. String a length of bright red or natural color raffia through the middle of a circular ornament or through the macaroni hole. Hang the decorations on an outdoor tree, from a window suction-cup holder, or a feeder support.

ATTRACTS

White-breasted Nuthatch   **Black-capped Chickadee**   **Downy Woodpecker**   **Evening Grosbeak**

NOTES

Birds have beaks uniquely structured to pick up, capture and open the foods they eat. Grosbeaks have big, bulky beaks that work like a pair of strong pliers to crack open hard seeds, including cherry pits. Look to the shape and length of a bird's beak for clues to what it eats. Their dinnerware possibilities include a spoon, fork, knife, straw, strainer, net, pliers, nutcracker, saw and chopsticks!

ALSO ATTRACTS: Red-headed, Red-bellied, Hairy and Pileated Woodpeckers; Yellow-bellied Sapsucker; Gray Catbird; Northern Mockingbird; Blue and Gray Jays; Eastern Towhee; Carolina and Mountain Chickadee; Tufted Titmouse

String popcorn, pasta loops and cranberries onto button thread in 4-foot lengths. Tie several lengths together and string around a tree outdoors. Make swags from millet or sorghum stems that are in full seed to decorate your outside windows and doors.

Gobbler Goulash

INGREDIENTS
4 cups of nuts: acorns,
   hickory nuts, peanuts
4 cups of cracked corn
4 cups of popped corn (hold the salt and butter)
Pasta Alfresco pieces (page 56), optional

TOOLS
Pail or large bowl

DIRECTIONS

STEP 1
Combine the nuts, cracked and popped corn, and pasta pieces in a pail or large bowl.

STEP 2
Before you place the goulash outside, consider making a tent-like wildlife-watching blind so that you can watch the birds by becoming a part of the habitat. Be resourceful and creative by using materials you have at home, like old sheets, blankets, or a tent.

STEP 3
Place your blind near existing cover rather than in the open. Camouflage your blind with natural materials similar to those in or near your backyard habitat.

STEP 4
Pour the goulash onto a raised ground feeder, or sprinkle part of the goulash directly on the ground.

STEP 5
Be aware of the time of day that wildlife are most likely to visit. Wild Turkeys venture to feeding areas like this at dawn, sunrise and at dusk. Position yourself in your hideout and watch for the fun to begin. Record your wildlife adventure in Chef Notes (page 84) and include drawings or photographs.

ATTRACTS

Wild
Turkey

Ring-necked
Pheasant

Northern
Bobwhite

Blue
Jay

NOTES

Wild Turkeys forage for food on the forest floor, where they find energy-rich nuts and seeds and protein-packed insects. If you live near a wooded area where Wild Turkeys live, you can invite them by providing the Gobbler Goulash in an open area with a brush pile on the edge, near trees or another edge near an open grassy area. When the goulash is left near a farm windbreak, or other edge near an open grassy area, Ring-necked Pheasants and Northern Bobwhites may come to feed. Get ready for ground-dwelling and nut-loving birds to gobble up this treat! Feeding turkeys can attract a large flock. Offering a smaller amount of food at staggered times often works to attract fewer birds.

ALSO ATTRACTS: Rock Pigeon; Chipping Sparrow; Mourning Dove; Wood Duck

Happy Bird-day Cake

INGREDIENTS

1 cup oatmeal, coarsely
   ground in food processor
¼ cup cornmeal
½ teaspoon baking powder
1 tablespoon Nyjer seed
1 tablespoon sunflower chips
1 egg
½ cup milk or water, warmed
2 tablespoons melted suet
⅓ cup Raisin-berry Relish (page 60), or raisins and cranberries
Toppings: peanut butter, nuts, seeds, carrot sticks and pumpkin seeds

TOOLS

Muffin tin and liners
Food processor

DIRECTIONS

STEP 1

Preheat the oven to 350°F. Line a muffin tin with paper liners. Set aside.

STEP 2

Combine the coarsely ground oatmeal, cornmeal, baking powder, seeds and sunflower chips in a medium mixing bowl. Make a well in the center.

STEP 3

Whip the egg in a separate bowl. Add the warmed milk or water, melted suet and then the Raisin-berry Relish.

STEP 4

Pour the egg mixture into the well in the center of the oatmeal-nut mixture. Stir until ingredients are combined, but do not overmix. Fill muffin cups ⅔ full.

STEP 5

Bake for 20 minutes or until lightly browned and a toothpick inserted in the center comes out clean. Cool. Frost with peanut butter and decorate with seeds, nuts and dried mealworms. Top with a carrot candle with a pumpkin-seed flame.

ATTRACTS

White-breasted
Nuthatch

Northern
Cardinal

Downy
Woodpecker

Evening
Grosbeak

NOTES

Celebrate the birds in your backyard with a cake. How many candles do birds have on their bird-day cake? For most birds, the first six months are the most perilous. In perching birds (Passerines), once the young have survived their first six months, they may have one, two, three, or as many as six birthdays. There are exceptional individual birds, however, like an American Robin that lived nearly 14 years!

ALSO ATTRACTS: Black-headed Grosbeak; Hairy Woodpecker; Blue Jay; Northern Mockingbird; Gray Catbird

This recipe can be divided into individual cake tins,
baked and frozen until needed.

Irresistible Insects

INGREDIENTS

Mealworms, mealworms,
mealworms

TOOLS

Cannonball gourd, mature
and dried
Length of rawhide or twine
Small craft saw
Drill

DIRECTIONS

STEP 1

To keep active mealworms in a feeder, it's best to use a container with sides that are at least 2 inches high. This can be the bottom of a clean coconut shell, the bottom of a gourd, or a clean recycled container.

STEP 2

If using a gourd feeder like the one pictured here, place cornmeal in the bottom of the feeder first, or simply place the worms on the bare surface. The feeder provides a roof that will shade the contents from direct sunlight.

STEP 3

To make a gourd feeder, first scrub the exterior of a mature, dried cannonball gourd with a copper kitchen scrubber and a strong solution of warm water and bleach. Dry.

STEP 4

Next, cut holes in the side so that the resulting base is about 2 inches deep. A small craft saw works well for this purpose. Clean out the inside of the gourd. Drill 3 small drainage holes in the bottom. Drill 2 holes in the top for threading a piece of rawhide or twine for use in hanging the gourd. Hang the feeder at a mid-level to lower level.

ATTRACTS

Brown
Creeper

Eastern
Bluebird

Chipping
Sparrow

Black-billed
Magpie

NOTES

New parents need all the help that they can get, especially when their chicks increase their mass by ten times in a mere ten days! To fuel this fast growth, many songbird parents feed their chicks mineral- and protein-packed insects. This can be a constant job, requiring some 15–20 trips per hour for a clutch of 4–6 chicks. Rose-breasted Grosbeaks make up to 50 food trips per hour to the nest! You can help songbird parents and the ravenous fledglings by providing a fast food café with mealworms—the Irresistible Insect Daily Special.

ALSO ATTRACTS: Yellow-rumped Warbler; Bushtit; Ovenbird; Eastern and Western Bluebird; Carolina Wren; House Wren; Ruby-crowned and Golden-crowned Kinglet; Indigo Bunting; Mountain Chickadee

You can buy live mealworms at pet supply stores, bait shops, bird feeding stores or online. Mealworms are the larval stage of the beetle Tenebrio molitor. *They stay alive for weeks in a refrigerator in a container with cornmeal for food and an apple slice for moisture. Place some holes in the top of the container, too.*

Jelly Deli

INGREDIENTS

3 cups grape juice
5¼ cups white sugar
1 package pectin (Sure-Jell)
¾ cup water
Fresh grapes

TOOLS

String or yarn, 2 feet
Small, recycled take-out
   coffee cup with lid

DIRECTIONS

STEP 1

Combine juice and sugar in a large bowl and mix well. Let stand 10 minutes.

STEP 2

Add the package of pectin to the water in a heavy saucepan and stir well. Heat this mixture on medium-high heat until it comes to a boil. Boil for 1 minute, stirring constantly. Remove from heat.

STEP 3

Pour the pectin mixture into the juice mixture and stir for about 3 minutes or until the grains of sugar are dissolved. Pour into plastic storage containers. Let the jelly set (become like a gel). This may take up to 24 hours. Freeze until needed. The jelly will keep for up to a year in the freezer.

STEP 4

Use the point of a pencil to make a hole in each side of the coffee cup, one-third of the way down from the lip of the cup. Insert the string through the holes. Tie the ends together at the top. Place tape over the holes.

STEP 5

Mix a dozen crushed fresh grapes with ½ cup of jelly and put in the coffee cup. Place the lid on the cup making certain that the drinking hole is open. This opening may be enlarged to make it easier for birds to get to the jelly. Avoid making sharp edges. The lid may be taped to the cup. Hang the jelly feeder from a tree branch (birds will need a perch while eating) by May 1st and watch for orioles, catbirds, robins and other birds to fill their belly with jelly!

ATTRACTS

American Robin   Baltimore Oriole   Blue Jay   Gray Catbird

male Baltimore Oriole

NOTES

Migratory songbirds often feed on fruit in their tropical wintering habitat. On their spring migration to North American nesting areas, they rest and eat during the day. Invite these bright birds to refuel their energy in your yard by setting out grape jelly loaded with fresh grapes and oranges by May 1st. After they fill their belly with jelly, they may even stay to nest in your neighborhood.

ALSO ATTRACTS: Northern Mockingbird; Eastern Towhee; White-breasted Nuthatch; Yellow-bellied Sapsucker; Summer Tanager

Krunchy Kabobs

INGREDIENTS

Fruit: any combination of
   apple, orange, cherry,
   prunes, large berries
   and/or fruits from
   ornamental trees or shrubs, like crabapples, and/or wild fruits
   like wild plums, cherries
Pasta Alfresco Pieces (page 56), Mockingbird Mini-muffins (page 50),
   and/or Woodpecker Waffle Pieces (page 70)

TOOLS

Wooden kabobs or skewers
String or yarn

DIRECTIONS

STEP 1

Hit the trail around your house and gather berries, ornamental cherries and crabapples, or use fruit that you already have on hand. Wash the fruit. If it is large, cut it into 1- to 2-inch cubes or slices. (Hint: The cut fruit must be large enough to stay together when inserted onto the kabob stick.)

STEP 2

Arrange a combination of fruit, pasta loops, mini-muffins, and/or 2-inch waffle pieces, to make a 6-inch chain on the table or counter. Then poke each piece onto the kabob stick, leaving enough room at the ends to tie a string.

STEP 3

Tightly tie the ends of a 16- to 20-inch length of string around each end of the kabob. Pipe cleaners can also be used. Add tape to the very ends so that the string will not slip off. The ends can also be set with glue to secure the string or pipe cleaner in place. (Hint: If you do not have kabob skewers, reuse your campfire marshmallow roasting sticks!)

STEP 4

Hang the treats from a tree branch or feeder support and watch for birds to kkkkrunch on kabobs!

ATTRACTS

Cedar
Waxwing

Gray
Jay

Summer
Tanager

American
Robin

NOTES

Birds that eat fruit take cues from color, texture and taste to determine when the fruit is at its peak in energy content (sugar). Some birds can see ultraviolet (UV) light. Many ripe fruits reflect UV light, but the leaves around them do not. This directs birds to the ripe fruit and a fast lunch. Plant fruit trees in your yard for a treat both you and wildlife can enjoy.

ALSO ATTRACTS: Northern Flicker; Northern Cardinal; Blue, Gray and Western Scrub Jays; Gray Catbird; Rose-breasted Grosbeak; Northern Mockingbird; Summer Tanager

Lunch Buddy

INGREDIENTS

1 pumpkin, melon or
  a large gourd
1 apple slice
2 grape halves (or other fruit
  to make eyes and mouth)
Tweet-tweet Trail Mix (page 64)

TOOLS

1 old pair of jeans or pants
1 old long-sleeved shirt
1 pair of old gloves
Recycled plastic shopping bags
Toothpicks
1 old hat (the best is one that
  is stiff, like a pillbox hat,
    western-style hat, top hat, etc.)
Basket

DIRECTIONS

STEP 1

Stuff the jeans, shirt and gloves with recycled plastic bags. Make a head with the gourd or pumpkin by using fruit on toothpicks for the eyes and nose, and the apple slice for a smiling mouth.

STEP 2

Place the hat on top of the gourd or pumpkin and put the trail mix on top.

STEP 3

Fill the buddy's hands and a bowl or basket with the trail mix. Place this on the lunch buddy's lap. In time, birds will get used to the buddy.

STEP 4

Sit quietly beside the lunch buddy. After the birds have eaten from their lunch buddy for some time, sit on the buddy's lap and hold the food-filled basket on your lap and the food in your hands. Sit very still and be quiet. Get ready—you will be the bird's lunch buddy too!

ATTRACTS

Black-capped Chickadee

Dark-eyed Junco

Song Sparrow

Chipping Sparrow

NOTES

Feeling the tiny feet of a chickadee on your finger while it eats seeds from your hand is incredible! It only takes patience, practice and following a few simple guidelines. Animals have a limited amount of energy and they need to use it to survive. As a rule, we are too close to wildlife when our presence changes their behavior and requires them to expend their valuable energy unnecessarily. When we become a natural part of their habitat, by way of motion, sound and visual cues, some birds become comfortable enough to allow us very near. Invite birds to dine with you and your backyard lunch buddy!

ALSO ATTRACTS: Golden-crowned, White-throated and White-crowned Sparrows; Mourning Dove; Rock Pigeon; Eastern and Spotted Towhee, Common Redpoll; Carolina and Mountain Chickadees

This is also a great opportunity to photograph, draw and journal about birds. For photography examples, visit the website (www.iwishicouldfly.com) of Alan Stankevitz, the wildlife photographer who took the recipe photos in this book.

Mockingbird Mini-muffins

INGREDIENTS

1½ cup cornmeal
¼ cup flour
1 tablespoon baking powder
1 cup of any combination of:
   cranberries, cherries,
   blueberries, raisins,
   or nuts and dried mealworms

1 egg
⅔ cup warm milk
⅓ cup melted suet

TOOLS

Mini-muffin pan
Mini-muffin cups
Raffia, twine, or string

DIRECTIONS

STEP 1

Preheat oven to 400°F. Place mini-muffin cups in the mini-muffin pan. In a bowl, mix together the cornmeal, flour, baking powder, and fruit, or mealworm and nuts, according to the season.

STEP 2

Break the egg into a separate bowl and mix well. Warm the milk in a microwave. Melt the suet in a microwave. Mix the egg, milk and suet until well blended.

STEP 3

Make a well in the middle of the cornmeal mixture. Pour the egg mixture into the center and stir all the ingredients together just until the cornmeal is moistened. It is ok if the batter is lumpy.

STEP 4

Fill each muffin cup ⅔ full with batter. Bake for 12–15 minutes or until golden brown. Remove from the oven and cool. Remove the paper from the muffins.

STEP 5

Make a small hook at the base of a pipe cleaner. Push the top of the pipe cleaner up through the bottom of the muffin so the long end comes through the top of the muffin. Hang the treats on plants or attach to a feeder support. Watch for mockingbirds, robins, catbirds and more to munch on your magnificent muffins.

ATTRACTS

Northern Mockingbird   Steller's Jay   Northern Cardinal   American Robin

NOTES

Mockingbirds can eat nearly anything. They eat insects, seeds, fruit and berries, depending on the season; they are omnivorous. During summer months they eat more insects and in the winter more fruit and berries. You can add seasonal favorites to these muffins. In winter, add cranberries, blueberries, raisins and cherries. In the summer, mix in extra protein—nuts and dried mealworms.

ALSO ATTRACTS: Mourning Dove; Gray Catbird; Black-headed Grosbeak; Blue Jay

Nectar Punch

INGREDIENTS
4 cups water
I cup white granulated sugar

TOOLS
Clean nectar feeder

DIRECTIONS

STEP 1

Measure the water and sugar into a heavy saucepan. There is no need to color the nectar. Artificial coloring agents have no nutritional value and do not enhance its attractiveness to them. Do not substitute honey or artificial sweeteners for the white sugar.

STEP 2

Heat the mixture on medium heat until it comes to a boil. Boil for one minute, stirring well to dissolve sugar. Remove from heat.

STEP 3

While the nectar is cooling, clean your nectar feeder and rinse it very well. (Hint: Nectar feeders need to be cleaned on a weekly basis. Cloudy nectar is a sign of bacterial growth, and the birds can become ill from it.)

STEP 4

Place your nectar feeder in a location with partial shade to discourage bacterial growth. During peak migration weeks, the nectar punch can be made more concentrated by reducing the ratio of water to sugar to 3:1. Hummingbirds love a water mister! Add a water mister or a source of clean dripping water to attract a variety of birds to your backyard or common areas.

ATTRACTS

Ruby-throated Hummingbird **Baltimore Oriole** **White-breasted Nuthatch** **Downy Woodpecker**

male Ruby-throated Hummingbird

NOTES

Hummingbirds feed from the nectar of up to 2,000 flowers per day to fuel their extraordinary output of energy—the most per unit of weight of any warm-blooded animal! Powered by wings that move in a unique figure-eight pattern, humming-birds fly forward, up, down, upside down, and claim the title as the only bird with the ability to fly backward. Their tiny body is as fluid as a fish and as muscular as an Olympic gymnast as they bend toward flower heads and weave aerial paths through gardens. A nectar feeder with fresh nectar provides these tiny wonders with instant energy.

ALSO ATTRACTS: Eastern Towhee; White-breasted and Red-breasted Nuthatches; Brown Creeper; Yellow-bellied Sapsucker; Anna's, Black-chinned and Rufous Hummingbird

The "hum" of the hummingbird is a result of the air movement from some 50–70 wingbeats per second. By way of comparison, most songbirds complete just 10–25 wingbeats per second during active flight.

Oriole Oranges

INGREDIENTS
Half an orange

TOOLS
Board, approximately 6-inches square and 1-inch thick
Nails, two #16
Hammer

DIRECTIONS

STEP 1
Pound one of the nails into what will be the back of the board, and drive it all the way through. The head of the nail should be flush with the back of the board.

STEP 2
Pound the second nail into the front of the board, just far enough into the board to create a perch.

STEP 3
Attach your fruit feeder to a vertical outdoor surface. Push an orange half onto the nail with the cut side facing out.

STEP 4 (OPTIONAL)
Once the orange half has been cleaned out by the birds, set the feeder flat and fill the orange rind cup with fresh or frozen peas and watch for parent orioles to take their chicks out for a green lunch. Other options include filling the cup with Raisin-berry Relish (page 60), or for seed-loving birds, Tweet-tweet Trail Mix (page 64).

To attract yet another group of birds, fill the orange rind with suet base, or pea-nutty or fruity suet, and place it back in the feeder. Now watch nuthatches, chickadees, woodpeckers and other birds fill up with energy!

ATTRACTS

Baltimore Oriole   **Red-bellied Woodpecker**   **Gray Catbird**   **Northern Mockingbird**

male Baltimore Oriole

NOTES

To attract fruit-loving birds to your backyard, make this simple fruit feeder, hang it outdoors and then watch for birds to munch on a free lunch. Provide year-round fruit by landscaping your yard with fruit-bearing plants: vines (Virginia creeper, wild grape, coral honeysuckle); shrubs (sumac, dogwood, nannyberry, serviceberry, elderberry); trees (cedar, juniper, wild plum, cherry).

ALSO ATTRACTS: American Robin; Yellow-bellied Sapsuckers; Red-headed Woodpecker; Bullock's Oriole

To view from indoors, screw a "screw-eye" into the top edge of the board. Then attach a suction-cup window hanger onto the outside of a window and hang the feeder from it.

Pasta Alfresco

INGREDIENTS

⅓ cup corn meal
¼ cup of proso millet (optional)
1 cup Masa corn flour
2 egg yolks (optional)
1 cup water

TOOLS

Rolling pin
Pizza cutter
Pasta machine (optional)

DIRECTIONS

STEP 1

Preheat oven to 375°F. Combine the first 2 ingredients in a mixing bowl and make a well in the center.

STEP 2

For egg noodles, add 2 egg yolks into the center and whisk with a fork, adding the water slowly. For plain pasta, omit the egg yolks and simply add the water.

STEP 3

Gradually bring the dry ingredients into the center until a ball forms. Use your hands to work the pasta dough into 4 balls.

STEP 4

Dust the counter top with corn flour and roll out the dough to the thickness of a nickel, or use a pasta machine. Cut and/or mold into desired pasta shapes. Make small donut shapes for using in Krunchy Kabobs (page 46), macaroni or shell shapes for Gobbler Goulash (page 38), and bill-size bites for Tweet-tweet Trail Mix (page 64). Brush the tops of the pasta pieces with a beaten egg and then sprinkle with proso millet seeds before baking.

STEP 5

Bake the pasta shapes for 10–15 minutes. Cool, and prepare for some extraordinary wildlife watching!

ATTRACTS

Rock
Pigeon

Mourning
Dove

Ring-necked
Pheasant

Wild
Turkey

NOTES

Watch pigeons long enough and you could count up to 28 different color types, or morphs! Pigeons even wear a necklace of bright iridescent purple, green and yellow feathers, called a hackle. They also have some very interesting behaviors. Count and record the different color morphs and note their behaviors to help scientists learn why pigeons can be found in so many different colors and which color morphs pigeons prefer for mates. Get to know your local ordinances about feeding pigeons and then check out the citizen science projects on page 25 for links to projects involving pigeons.

ALSO ATTRACTS: Northern Mockingbird; Rose-breasted and Black-headed Grosbeaks; Blue Jay

Quacker Crackers

INGREDIENTS

½ cup cornmeal
1 cup of oatmeal
   (moderately ground in
   food processor)
¼ cup melted suet base
½ cup water

TOOLS

Pizza cutter
Baking sheet
Hot pad

DIRECTIONS

STEP 1
Preheat the oven to 400°F.

STEP 2
Combine the cornmeal, finely ground oatmeal, melted suet and water.

STEP 3
Roll the dough with a rolling pin until thin, about the thickness of a quarter.

STEP 4
With a pizza cutter, cut the dough into 1-inch x 1-inch squares, or be creative and make your own bird-sized cracker shapes with mini-cookie cutters. Prick the cracker tops with the tines of a fork.

STEP 5
Bake for 10–12 minutes. Remove from the oven. Cool.

ATTRACTS

| Mallard | American Black Duck | Canada Goose | Wood Duck |

NOTES

Gritty, grainy, smooth, hard or juicy, when a bird decides to eat one food over another, it has more to do with texture than taste. Birds generally have few taste buds and a poor sense of taste, but their tongue has a detailed system of sensors that allows them to tell food items apart. Add to the menu by landscaping with natural plants that provide migratory birds food throughout the year. In rural areas, plant rows of corn, sorghum and other grains for migratory birds. The plants will also provide winter cover for local wildlife. Also, when feeding ducks be aware that one duck can attract many others, so be sure to check your local ordinances, which sometimes prohibit feeding of waterfowl.

ALSO ATTRACTS: Rock Pigeon; Mourning Dove; Eastern and Spotted Towhees; Chipping Sparrow

Take along a sketchbook and/or camera to record your waterside adventures. Can you determine male, female, adult and young birds from each other? Take notes on their behaviors, too.

Raisin-berry Relish

INGREDIENTS

½ cup orange juice
1 cup raisins or currants
1 10-ounce package (about 3 cups)
   of fresh or frozen cranberries
1 cup brown sugar

TOOLS

Half of an orange rind, or
   another serving container

DIRECTIONS

STEP 1

Pour the orange juice over the raisins, cranberries and sugar in a heavy sauce-pan. Stir well. Heat the mixture on medium-high until it starts to bubble. Carefully stir the hot mixture.

STEP 2

Turn down the heat to low and put a cover on the pan. Simmer for 30 minutes or until the berries pop. Remove from the heat and cool.

STEP 3

Be creative with your food presentation. There are many options of how to offer this treat to birds. Fill empty orange halves with the mixture (Oriole Oranges, page 54). Make surprise muffins: Fill the mini-muffin cups one-third full with Mockingbird Mini-muffin batter (page 50); next, place a teaspoon of relish on the batter, and then fill the muffin cup the remaining two-thirds full with batter. Bake as directed. For a simple presentation, place the relish in a clean, empty 6-ounce tuna can and set outside in a predator-free area.

STEP 4

For a no-cook relish, soak the raisins and cranberries in orange juice overnight or until they are plump. Add chopped apples to the relish.

ATTRACTS

Northern
Cardinal

Eastern
Bluebird

Cedar Waxwing

Steller's
Jay

male Baltimore Oriole

NOTES

In the wild, birds spend large amounts of energy foraging for food. The availability of fruit is seasonal, especially in the North. Backyard bird feeding provides birds with a wide variety of foods all year long, and scientists are still researching how much of an advantage birds receive from this type of feeding. The effects of global warming are being researched as well. Set out this fruit-filled relish and note the date, time and numbers of bird species that come to dine. Report your findings to a citizen science project (page 25) and be a part of solving the mysteries!

ALSO ATTRACTS: Bohemian Waxwing; American Robin; Red-bellied Woodpecker; Summer Tanager; Baltimore Oriole; Gray Catbird; Brown Thrasher; White-crowned Sparrow

Sunflower Snack

INGREDIENTS

1 Woodpecker
   Waffle (page 70)
1 orange
¼ cup peanut butter
½ cup striped sunflower seeds
¼ cup black oil sunflower seeds

TOOLS

Biscuit cutter
8 toothpicks
12 inches of ribbon

DIRECTIONS

STEP 1

With a biscuit cutter, cut a circle from a waffle. Poke a small hole about one-third of the way from an edge. Pull the ribbon through the hole and tie it at the ends to make a closed loop. (Hint: Placing a piece of elbow macaroni or a small section of a drinking straw in the hole first and then passing the string through it adds extra support.)

STEP 2

Arrange the toothpicks equally around the outside edge of the waffle, pushing them in about half way. Peel an orange and set out 4 to 8 sections. Use the sections whole or cut the 4 sections in half to make eight sunflower petals. Place one section on each toothpick.

STEP 3

Spread peanut butter on the waffle section, covering entire surface to the edges.

STEP 4

Arrange overlapping rings of striped sunflower seeds around the outside of the center section, pressing them firmly into place. Fill in the center with black oil sunflower seeds. Hang the sunflower snack in your garden and birds will learn where snacks are found while your sunflower garden grows!

ATTRACTS

Northern
Cardinal

Blue
Jay

Evening
Grosbeak

Rose-breasted
Grosbeak

NOTES

Plant one sunflower seed in your garden in the spring and the birds will have hundreds of sunflower seeds to snack on at the end of the summer. Plant six sunflower seeds in a 4-foot-diameter circle. When they have grown to full height, tie the tops together below the blossoms. The reading room in the center is just the place to enjoy the birds while you read! While your wildlife garden grows, make this bird snack.

ALSO ATTRACTS: Black-headed Grosbeak; White-breasted and Red-breasted Nuthatches; Northern Flicker; Black-billed Magpie

Tweet-tweet Trail Mix

INGREDIENTS
1 cup cranberries
1 cup raisins
1 cup oatmeal
1 cup cornmeal
1 cup raw, unsalted peanuts
1 cup black oil sunflower seeds,
1 cup striped sunflower seeds
1 cup safflower seeds
1 cup peanut hearts

TOOLS
1-gallon bucket or large bowl

DIRECTIONS

STEP 1
Mix all ingredients together in a bucket or container.

STEP 2
Use this mix to fill backyard feeders (Coconut Café, page 30; Lunch Buddy, page 48) and as an extra ingredient in suet base (1 part mix to 2 parts suet base).

STEP 3
You can make this mix in large quantities to use throughout the year. Seeds need to be kept in a sealed and rodent-proof container such as a metal garbage can with a lid or another similar container.

ATTRACTS

Eastern
Towhee

Fox
Sparrow

White-crowned
Sparrow

Mourning
Dove

Blue Jay

NOTES

The food you set out in the fall may disappear from your feeder, but it may not necessarily be directly eaten by backyard birds. Some species store the nuts and seeds for eating during the coldest days of the year when their energy needs are the highest. Research indicates that during the fall, species such as chickadees can produce new brain cells to handle the additional memory they need to recover the cached food in winter. They probably do not remember where every seed is hidden, and that allows other wildlife to benefit from this store of winter food.

ALSO ATTRACTS: Spotted Towhee; Rock Pigeon; White-throated and Golden-crowned Sparrows; Northern Cardinal, Common Redpoll, Pine Grosbeak

Squirrels like the same foods as backyard birds and can devour the supply in short order. If you enjoy watching and feeding squirrels, you can set up separate corn feeders just for them. You can discourage squirrels by placing bird feeders away from trees and putting squirrel guards on standing feeders.

Ultimate Finch Feeder

INGREDIENTS
Nyjer seeds

TOOLS
Stretchy nylon or sock
Length of string or twine

DIRECTIONS

STEP 1

Find a pair of women's nylons or a pair of socks that are stretchy enough to extend the mesh. Cut the bottom end of the nylon or sock to a length of 10–12 inches.

STEP 2

Fill the sock about half to three-quarters full with Nyjer seeds.

STEP 3

Fold the open end over and then tie a rubber band tightly around it. Next, secure a large, heavy safety pin through the layers at the end. Tie the open end of the stocking together in a knot. Place a length of twine, string, or yarn through the middle of the knot with enough length to hang the feeder from a tree branch or feeder support.

STEP 4

Punching a few small pencil holes in the stocking mesh may make it easier for finches to pick out the seed.

ATTRACTS

Purple Finch

American Goldfinch

House Finch

White-throated Sparrow

male House Finch and female American Goldfinch

NOTES

American Goldfinches and raspberry-colored Purple Finches use their cone-shaped bill to break open seeds. The most popular wild seed among finches is the small, black Nyjer seed. Watch as a finch adeptly pinches a seed from the feeder with its bill, like a tiny pair of tweezers, and then maneuvers the seed with its bill and tongue to break it open at just the right spot. Have a pair of binoculars handy for a close-up view of this fascinating feeder frenzy.

ALSO ATTRACTS: Cassin's Finch; Lesser Goldfinch; Tufted Titmouse; Pine Siskin; Common Redpoll

Thistle seeds that fall to the ground provide food for Mourning Doves, Dark-eyed Juncos, Song Sparrows and White-throated Sparrows.

Veggie Vittles

INGREDIENTS

1 ear of fresh sweet corn
Fresh or frozen peas
Pumpkin or squash seeds,
   fresh or dried

TOOLS

2 feet of string or yarn
Toothpicks

DIRECTIONS

STEP 1

Take off all husk and silk from a fresh ear of sweet corn. Leave the stem attached. Wash the corn.

STEP 2

Make a hole through the stem of the corn large enough for a piece of string or yarn to pass through. Feed the string through the hole and tie at the ends.

STEP 3

Poke the peas and seeds onto the toothpicks. To make this easier, the seeds can be soaked in water for up to 30 minutes ahead of time.

STEP 4

Poke the toothpicks into the ear of corn. (Hint: The toothpicks need to be pointing upward, toward the stem of the corn.)

STEP 5

Hang the corn from a feeder support or tree branch and watch for birds to vie for vittles.

ATTRACTS

Northern
Mockingbird

Northern
Flicker

Red-bellied
Woodpecker

Blue
Jay

NOTES

Birds that migrate long distances in the fall need extra energy for their journey. The decrease of sunlight in late summer triggers a bird's body to produce hormones (body chemicals) that stimulate them to eat more and put on extra stores of fat. This fat is what provides the energy for their long journey. You can provide foods like fresh corn that have nutrients and plenty of calories for migratory birds that are bulking up. Bring on the vittles!

ALSO ATTRACTS: Yellow-bellied Sapsucker; Gray Catbird; Northern Cardinal; Rose-breasted Grosbeak

Consider purchasing the slightly more expensive blunt-ended wooden cocktail picks. These could be easier on the birds should they get poked.

Woodpecker Waffles

INGREDIENTS

2 eggs
1 cup milk, warmed
¼ cup melted suet
1½ cups cornmeal
2 teaspoons baking powder
¼ cup chopped walnuts
¼ cup suet or peanut butter
¼ cup safflower seeds or peanut hearts

TOOLS

Waffle iron

DIRECTIONS

STEP 1

Preheat the waffle iron according to the manufacturer's directions. Break 2 eggs into a medium-sized bowl and whip with a wire whisk. Add the warm milk and melted suet. Mix thoroughly. (Hint: Warming the milk will keep the melted suet from cooling and turning hard.)

STEP 2

In a large mixing bowl, stir together the cornmeal, baking powder and nuts.

STEP 3

Make a well in the center of the dry ingredients. Pour the wet ingredients into the center. Stir until the mixture is well blended. There will be a few lumps.

STEP 4

Spoon enough batter for 1 waffle onto the preheated waffle iron. Cook the waffle until it is well done and dark brown, but not burnt. (Hint: This recipe works best when the waffles are very stiff. This may take 2 or more pre-set heat cycles.)

STEP 5

Fill the square spaces of the cooled waffle with suet or peanut butter and sprinkle with safflower seeds or peanut hearts, or place a large striped sunflower seed in each square hole. Generally, two waffles back-to-back will fill a typical wire mesh suet feeder.

ATTRACTS

Red-bellied Woodpecker   Hairy Woodpecker   Downy Woodpecker   Red-headed Woodpecker

Hairy Woodpecker

NOTES

Woodpeckers and other hearty birds that live in the north all year keep up their heat-producing energy by eating winter foods high in fat and carbohydrates. Fill the square "holes" in these waffles with suet or peanut butter and then sprinkle another high-energy layer of nut meats on the top. Watch for birds to go wacky over your waffles!

ALSO ATTRACTS: Red-breasted and White-breasted Nuthatches; Black-billed Magpie; Tufted Titmouse; Northern Flicker; Black-capped, Carolina and Mountain Chickadees

Xtra Pea-nutty Parfait

INGREDIENTS

1 cup suet base
¾ cup crunchy peanut butter
shelled and unshelled
   peanuts, unsalted

TOOLS

Ice cream scoop
Parfait glass or recycled dish

DIRECTIONS

STEP 1

Warm suet in a microwave until soft, but not entirely melted. Combine suet base with ½ cup crunchy peanut butter. Mix well.

STEP 2

Place 1 or more scoops of suet mixture in the center of a parfait dish or recycled bowl.

STEP 3

Melt the remaining ¼ cup peanut butter in a microwave. (Hint: this will only take about three, 10-second intervals.) Drizzle the melted peanut butter over the top of the suet ball.

STEP 4

Top with shelled and unshelled peanuts or peanut hearts. Optional toppings: crushed eggshell, a cherry (not maraschino) and squirmy mealworms.

STEP 5

Place the pea-nutty parfait on a tree stump or other elevated stand near tree branches (but not accessible to roaming cats and squirrels). Watch for nut-hatches, jays and woodpeckers as they go nutty over this scrumptious snack.

ATTRACTS

White-breasted Nuthatch   Red-breasted Nuthatch   Blue Jay   Downy Woodpecker

Blue Jay

NOTES

Peanuts are a powerhouse of protein. They are also a source of vitamins B and E, and minerals such as magnesium, copper, phosphorus, potassium and zinc. Birds are the only animal on earth with feathers. Feathers are made of keratin, which is nearly all protein. Growing new feathers requires nutrients and protein. Provide peanuts to birds especially during late summer, when many molt (lose old feathers and grow new ones). Pass the peanuts, please.

ALSO ATTRACTS: Tufted Titmouse; Carolina, Black-capped and Mountain Chickadees; Yellow-bellied Sapsucker; Hairy, Red-headed and Red-bellied Woodpeckers

Yum-yum Nachos

INGREDIENTS
Pasta Alfresco dough (page 56)
Raisin-berry Relish (page 60)
6-ounces of mild cheddar
    cheese, cubed or
    shredded
Mealworms, optional garnish

TOOLS
Rolling pin
Baking sheet
Hot pad
Cheese grater or knife
Recycled container or old plate

DIRECTIONS

STEP 1
Preheat oven to 375°F. Prepare the pasta dough according to the directions on page 56. Roll the dough to ¼-inch thick. Cut the rolled dough into rounds with the drinking edge of a small juice glass or a 2-inch jar lid. (Hint: Dipping the cutting edge in cornmeal first may prevent the edge or lid from sticking to the dough.)

STEP 2
Place the nacho rounds onto a greased cookie sheet. Bake for 8–10 minutes or until the tops and bottoms are browned. Remove from the oven and let cool.

STEP 3
Cut the cheese into small (¼-inch) cubes, or grate the cheese using the largest holes in the cheese grater. Set aside.

STEP 4
Place a spoonful of Raisin-berry Relish on top of the nacho round. Sprinkle cheese on the top. Mealworms can also be sprinkled on the top.

STEP 5
Put the nacho rounds on a recycled plate (heavy enough to withstand wind) and place on a tree stump or another elevated stand. Yum-yum, here they come for this nutritious nacho treat.

ATTRACTS

Rose-breasted Grosbeak   Gray Jay   Northern Flicker   Northern Mockingbird

NOTES

Setting the table in your yard involves placing food at different levels of your backyard habitat. Birds that feed in trees will utilize feeders set at higher levels: nuthatches, woodpeckers, titmice, finches, chickadees and jays. Birds like cardinals that inhabit mid-level shrubs will visit mid-level feeders. Likewise, birds that naturally pick and glean foods from the ground will visit lower and ground-level feeders. Set your yard for success and enjoy the wide variety of birds that come to dine.

ALSO ATTRACTS: Gray Catbird; Red-bellied Woodpecker; Black-headed Grosbeak; Baltimore Oriole

Zebra-striped Suet-sicles

INGREDIENTS
3 cups of suet, melted
1 cup Nyjer seed

TOOLS
Popsicle mold or small
    paper cups
Popsicle sticks or crafts sticks
String, yarn, twine, or raffia

DIRECTIONS

STEP 1
Place the popsicle mold or paper cups on a baking sheet with wax paper underneath. Set out a bowl of Nyjer seed seeds. Lay out the popsicle or craft sticks. Drill a hole through each stick, near the end. (Hint: Some craft sticks come with holes already made.)

STEP 2
Melt 1 cup of suet in a glass measuring cup in the microwave.

STEP 3
Pour 1 inch of melted suet into each cup or popsicle mold. Place in the refrigerator for about 10 minutes, or until the suet just starts to cool. Sprinkle a layer of thistle seeds into the partially cooled suet. Push the sticks into the centers of the suet-sicles, keeping the ends with the holes on top. Place back in the refrigerator to cool for about 10 more minutes.

STEP 4
Repeat steps 2 and 3 until the mold is full. Chill until hard. Pop the suet-sicles from the mold. If they don't release easily, place the mold in warm water for 30 seconds.

STEP 5
Place a 12-inch length of string, yarn, twine, or raffia through the hole in the suet-sicle stick and tie the two ends together in a slip knot. Hang the zebra-striped suet-sicles from a tree branch, feeder support, or suction-cup window hanger. Watch for woodpeckers, chickadees and other birds to zip in for a suet-sicle treat.

ATTRACTS

Black-capped
Chickadee

Red-breasted
Nuthatch

Tufted
Titmouse

Downy
Woodpecker

NOTES

Providing suet, seeds and nuts to backyard birds during the winter offers the fats and carbohydrates needed to fuel their internal furnace. The smaller the bird, the greater its surface-area to volume ratio. This requires proportionally more fuel in the way of food consumption. Blue Jays need to eat about 10% of their body weight in food per day, but the much smaller chickadees need to eat about 35% of their body weight in food per day. Bring on the suet-sicles!

ALSO ATTRACTS: White-breasted Nuthatch; Hairy Woodpecker; Carolina and Mountain Chickadees

Birds You Can Attract

Each recipe page in this book includes lists of bird species that may be attracted to the recipe. All of the species listed on the recipe pages are depicted here, along with their general geographical range. Since local populations of particular species vary significantly, note that some bird species may be more prevalent than others. Whichever birds show up, these photos should help you start identifying the species attracted to your recipes. As bird species can look alike and be hard to distinguish, it's best to refer to a field guide to help you definitively identify birds.

American Black Duck
East/West

American Goldfinch
East/West

American Robin
East/West

Baltimore Oriole
East

Black-billed Magpie
West

Black-capped Chickadee
East/West

Blue Jay
East/West

Brown Creeper
North

Canada Goose
East/West

Cedar Waxwing
East

Chipping Sparrow
East/West

Dark-eyed Junco
East/West

Downy Woodpecker
East/West

Eastern Bluebird
East

Eastern Towhee
East

Birds You Can Attract (continued)

Evening Grosbeak
East/West

Fox Sparrow
East/West

Gray Catbird
East/West

Gray Jay
North

Hairy Woodpecker
East/West

House Finch
East/West

House Wren
East

Mallard
East/West

Mourning Dove
East/West

Northern Bobwhite
North/East

Northern Cardinal
East/West

Northern Flicker
East/West

Northern Mockingbird
East/West

Purple Finch
East/West

Purple Martin
East/West

Red-bellied Woodpecker
East

Red-breasted Nuthatch
East/West

Red-headed Woodpecker
East/West

Birds You Can Attract (continued)

Ring-necked Pheasant
East/West

Rock Pigeon
East/West

Rose-breasted Grosbeak
East

Ruby-throated Hummingbird
East

Song Sparrow
East/West

Steller's Jay
West

Summer Tanager
South

Tufted Titmouse
East

White-breasted Nuthatch
East/West

White-crowned Sparrow
East/West

White-throated Sparrow
East

Wild Turkey
East/West

Wood Duck
East/West

Yellow-rumped Warbler
East/West

Chef Notes

Chef Notes

Chef Notes

Chef Notes

87

About the Author

Award-winning author and science educator Adele Porter combines her passion for science and dedication to children in her new books. In fact, the students that Adele has worked with during 20 years as an educator inspired the *Wild About* series of books. Adele has also written educational materials for the Minnesota Department of Natural Resources, the U.S. Forest Service and various publications. She is a member of the National Science Teachers' Association, the American Ornithologists' Union and the Society of Children's Book Writers and Illustrators.

REFERENCES

Poole, A. (Editor). *The Birds of North America Online:* http://bna.birds.cornell.edu/BNA/. Cornell Laboratory of Ornithology: Ithaca, 2005.

Henderson, Carrol L. *Wild About Birds: The DNR Bird Feeding Guide.* Minnesota's Bookstore: St. Paul, 1995.